VEGAN DESSERTS FOR

BEGINNERS

A Step-By-Step Guide To Delicious and Easy Homemade vegan
Desserts that are Delicious and Soul Satisfying

SUSY RYES

indirect, which are incurred as a result of the use of information contained within this document, including, but not limited to, — errors, omissions, or inaccuracies.

TABLE OF CONTENTS

1. CARROT CAKE SMOOTHIE

Indulge at breakfast time with this delish drink! It boasts the addition of blackstrap molasses, which is chock full of good stuff like copper, iron, calcium, and potassium.

1 large carrot, stems and top removed

1 large banana, peeled and frozen

3 dates

½ cup unsweetened almond milk

¾ cup cold water

½ teaspoon cinnamon

Dash nutmeg

Dash cloves

1 teaspoon blackstrap molasses

Place the first four ingredients in a blender and process until the banana is mostly blended. Add the water, spices, and molasses and blend until creamy. Thin to taste with additional cold water, if desired. Serve immediately.

2. PIÑA COLADA

YIE
LD:
2
SER
VIN
GS

This tastes so authentic you may expect to feel a bit tipsy while sipping; but, rest assured, this libation is quite good for you. It may even ward off colds with all that pineapple, which is very high in vitamin C!

1 large peeled frozen banana

⅛ cup coconut cream (from can of coconut milk)

4 pineapple rings (or about ½ cup canned pineapple)

¾ cup pineapple juice

1 teaspoon rum extract

- Blend all ingredients until very smooth in a high-speed blender. Serve immediately.

3. HAPPY HEALTHY HOT COCOA

This hot cocoa will leave you feeling happy and healthy after sipping as it's sweetened with date sugar and stevia, rather than the usual refined sugar mixture. I like this best made with unsweetened almond milk.

3 tablespoons cocoa powder

¼ cup date sugar

¼ teaspoon pure liquid stevia

1 teaspoon vanilla or almond extract

1 cup unsweetened non dairy milk, plus more to thin

- In a blender, combine the cocoa powder, date sugar, stevia, vanilla extract, and ½ cup almond milk. Blend on high speed until very smooth, adding the additional ½ cup almond milk as it becomes more blended. You should have a very thick, creamy, chocolate syrup.

- Thin with a little more non dairy milk until desired consistency and heat over medium heat, until warm, stirring constantly. For an extra-special treat, top with Sweetened Whipped Coconut Cream, stevia version. Serve immediately.

4. APPLE PIE MILKSHAKE

YIELD: 1 SERVING

Easier than apple pie, and good for you, too! This "milk shake" makes a perfectly indulgent breakfast or a late afternoon snack.

1½ bananas, chopped and frozen

⅔ cup apple cider (no sugar added)

⅓ cup pecans

½ teaspoon cinnamon

Dash nutmeg

- Combine all ingredients into a blender and mix until very smooth. Thin with a little extra apple cider or nondairy milk if desired.

- Serve immediately.

5. CHOCOLATE GRANOLA

This versatile granola is perfect for all sorts of treats: Use for parfaits or to top your favorite non dairy yogurt or ice cream. Great in a bowl as breakfast cereal at home, or as a chocolaty addition to your trail mix when you're on the go.

2 cups certified gluten-free oats

⅓ cup almond meal

3 tablespoons whole chia seed

¼ teaspoon salt

⅓ cup cocoa powder

1 tablespoon coconut oil

1 teaspoon vanilla extract

⅓ cup agave or maple syru

- Preheat oven to 300°F. In a medium bowl, whisk

together the oats, almond meal, chia seed, salt, and cocoa powder. In a smaller bowl, whisk together the coconut oil, vanilla extract, and maple syrup until very smooth. Using clean hands, or a large fork, combine all ingredients until well mixed. Spread onto a parchment-lined jelly roll pan and bake for 40 minutes. Break into bite-size pieces and let cool completely. Store in airtight container for up to 3 weeks.

6. SWEET, SALTY, AND SOFT GRANOLA BARS

YIELD: 12 BARS

With its salty, sweet flavor and soft, chewy texture, this snack can satisfy multiple cravings at once! Store in an airtight container in the refrigerator for best texture.

2½ cups certified gluten-free oats

½ cup almond meal

1 teaspoon salt

2 tablespoons maple syrup

⅓ cup agave

¼ cup + 2 tablespoons softened coconut oil

¼ cup date sugar or coconut palm sugar

1 teaspoon vanilla extract

½ cup sliced almonds

1 tablespoon ground chia seed

3 tablespoons water

- Preheat oven to 350°F. Lightly grease an 8 × 8-inch pan.

- Spread the oats in an even layer onto a large baking sheet and lightly toast for 7 minutes. Remove oats from the oven and place them in a large mixing bowl. Using your hands, crumble in the almond meal, salt, maple syrup, agave, coconut oil, date sugar, vanilla extract, and sliced almonds.

- Mix the chia seed and water and let rest for 5 minutes, until gelled. Mix in with the rest of the ingredients and then using hands lightly greased with coconut oil, press the mixture tightly and firmly into the pan. Cover lightly with plastic wrap and refrigerate for 2 hours. Gently cut into bars and store chilled in

7. POWERHOUSE BARS

With goji berries, hemp seeds, chia seed, and oats, these protein-packed bars are full of all kinds of nourishing ingredients that will keep you going strong all day long.

1 cup pecans

½ cup raw cashews

9 dates

¼ teaspoon salt

1 tablespoon coconut oil

½ cup certified gluten-free oats

½ cup goji berries

¼ cup hemp seeds

¼ cup chia seed

- Line an 8 × 8-inch baking pan with plastic wrap or lightly oil with coconut oil.

- Place the pecans, cashews, and five of the dates into a food processor and blend until evenly crumbly. Add the salt and the remaining dates and pulse until well combined and dates are evenly chopped. Transfer mixture into a large bowl and stir in the coconut oil to evenly coat. Fold in the oats, goji berries, hemp seeds, and chia seed. Press the mixture firmly into the prepared baking pan and refrigerate for 2 hours. Cut into bars and store in an airtight container in the refrigerator for up to 2 weeks.

8. EASY HOLIDAY BARK

YIELD: 8 SERVINGS

A surefire way to impress without any additional holiday stress! Add in your favorite candies from the holiday, or stick to the traditional version as I have below. Either way, you'll end up with a treat good enough to gift.

2 cups non dairy dark chocolate, coins or chips

2 cups non dairy white chocolate, chunks or chips

1 cup crushed candy canes (check ingredients for gluten or animal products)

- Have an 8 × 8-inch silicone pan ready to go. You can also use a baking sheet lined with waxed paper or aluminum foil, but silicone is best.

- Over a double boiler, melt or temper (instructions) the dark chocolate and spread evenly into the silicone baking pan. Place the chocolate in the refrigerator to firm up.

- In the meantime, prepare the white chocolate by melting over a double boiler. Depending on what type of chocolate you are using, it could be totally liquid, or very thick. Once melted, spread or pour the white chocolate on top of the solidified dark chocolate. Sprinkle with crushed candy canes. Let harden and then score into pieces. Store in airtight container for up to 1 month.

9. CHOCOLATE PEPPERMINT PATTIES

This candy takes the classic peppermint patty one step further and infuses it with an extra-intense chocolate flavor. If you cannot locate the dark cocoa powder, regular cocoa powder will work well. You can use an equal amount of Sweet Cashew Cream in place of the vegan cream cheese for a soy-free version.

2 cups confectioners sugar

¼ cup dark cocoa powder

¼ cup + 2 tablespoons non dairy cream cheese

½ teaspoon sea salt

1 teaspoon peppermint extract

2 cups non dairy semi-sweet chocolate

- In a large mixing bowl (an electric mixer works best), combine the confectioner's sugar, cocoa powder, cream cheese, salt, and peppermint extract until very smooth. Divide into two equal disks and wrap in waxed paper. Chill in the refrigerator for at least 1 hour, or for 10 to 15 minutes in the freezer.

- Place one disk of chocolate dough between two sheets of parchment and roll until about ¼ inch thick. Use a 1½-inch round cookie cutter to cut out circles. Place circles of dough back into the fridge and let chill while you melt the chocolate.

- Over a double boiler on medium-low heat, melt the chocolate until shiny and smooth, or temper according to directions on tempering. Coat the disks of chilled dough by painting on the chocolate with a pastry brush. Gently place onto a waxed paper–lined wire rack to cool. Let set until chocolate is firm. Store in refrigerator in airtight container for up to 1 month.

10. DOUBLE CHOCOLATE CARAMEL BARS

YIELD: ABOUT 4 CANDY BARS

These candy bars are filled with an irresistible chocolate-caramel filling that just begs you to take one more bite. These full-size candy bars can be made into small chocolate caramels by using a smaller mold. Looking for a lighter flavor? Try these with white chocolate chips in the filling instead of the three additional tablespoons of dark chocolate.

1 cup plus 3 tablespoons non dairy couverture coins or chips

2 tablespoons non dairy margarine or coconut oil

2½ cups vegan marshmallows, such as Dandies or Sweet and Sara

- Using the tempering instructions in this book, temper the 1 cup of the chocolate. Coat the inside of four standard-size candy bar molds with three-quarters of the chocolate. Let the chocolate set completely for about 1 hour.

- In a small saucepan over medium-low heat, melt the margarine along with the 3 tablespoons chocolate coins. Add in the marshmallows and stir constantly until completely melted, for about 1 to 2 minutes.

- Let cool for about 5 minutes and then fill the chocolate molds with filling. Cover with the rest of the tempered chocolate and use a straight edge to flatten completely. Let candy bars set completely, for about 2 hours, or until they easily release from the molds. Store in cool, dry place, wrapped or unwrapped in airtight container for up to 1 week.

11. CREAM EGGS

These are so easy to make, you just need a good chocolate mold (clear plastic) and an afternoon with nothing going on. The food coloring isn't needed in this recipe but helps create the authentic "yolk" we've grown so accustomed to in a cream egg.

1 egg-shaped plastic chocolate mold that fits twenty chocolate egg halves

2¼ cups couverture chocolate, divided

¼ cup light corn syrup

2 tablespoons non dairy margarine, softened

1 cup confectioners sugar

1 teaspoon vanilla extract

1 to 2 drops yellow food coloring

- Over a double boiler, temper 2 cups of the chocolate according to the directions on tempering. Coat the insides of twenty plastic chocolate molds shaped like egg halves. You can also use a typical truffle-style mold and coat each cavity evenly with chocolate. Let chocolate harden completely and then make the filling.

- To make the filling, in a small bowl whisk together the corn syrup, margarine, confectioner's sugar, and vanilla extract until very smooth. Transfer one-quarter of the filling into a separate bowl and add in the yellow food coloring.

- Pop out the egg shapes from the mold.

- Fill ten of the chocolate egg cavities two-thirds of the way full with the white filling and then drop a central spot of yellow fondant into the center of the white to fill almost full, leaving a little room at the top so the fondant doesn't over-flow. Temper ¼ cup of the remaining chocolate and pipe the chocolate onto just the edges of one of the eggs; use to glue each half of the eggs together, one filled and one hollow. Let chocolate harden completely. Store in cool dry place for up to 3 weeks.

12.   TIRAMISU

Tiramisu is perhaps one of the most popular desserts at Italian restaurants. I always love Tiramisu for its intoxicating fragrance and delightfully melt-in- your-mouth texture. After going gluten-free, I was convinced this dessert would be off limits for good, but no more! Allergy-friendly fancy dessert, at your service.

10 to 12 Ladyfingers

¼ recipe Devilishly Dark Chocolate Sauce

FILLING

1 recipe Mascarpone

1½ cups confectioner's sugar

⅛ teaspoon salt

12 ounces firm silken tofu

3 ounces (about 3 tablespoons) non dairy cream cheese

3 tablespoons cornstarch

4 tablespoons cold water

SAUCE

1 tablespoon cocoa powder, plus more for dusting

1 tablespoon agave

2 tablespoons very strong coffee or espresso

For the Filling

- Place the Mascarpone, confectioner's sugar, salt, tofu, and nondairy cream cheese into a food processor and blend until very smooth, for about 2 minutes. Transfer the mixture into a 2-quart saucepan over medium heat.

- Whisk together the cornstarch and cold water until no lumps remain. Drizzle the cornstarch slurry into the rest of the ingredients and whisk together, continuing to cook over medium heat. Keep stirring continuously until the mixture thickens, for about 5 minutes. Do not walk away from the mixture or it will burn!

- Let cool briefly.

For the Sauce

- Prepare the sauce by whisking together the cocoa powder, agave, and coffee in a small bowl until smooth.

To assemble the Tiramisu

- In a small, square baking pan, arrange five or six ladyfinger cookies to fit into the pan. Spread the Cocoa Espresso Sauce into a shallow flat dish, big enough for the cookies to lay flat. One by one, dip each side of the cookie into the sauce, briefly, and carefully replace. Repeat until all the cookies have been lightly dipped.

- Divide the Tiramisu filling in half and spread half of the filling on top of the ladyfingers and repeat with one more layer of each. Dust the top with cocoa powder and then drizzle with the Devilishy Dark Chocolate Sauce right before serving. Store in airtight container for up to 3 days in refrigerator.

13. BROWNIE BATTER MOUSSE

Tiny bites of chocolate-covered walnuts—that taste a heck of a lot like miniature brownies—speckle this silky mousse, delivering a double dose of chocolate flavor.

6 ounces chopped semi-sweet chocolate

2 tablespoons non dairy milk

1 tablespoon maple syrup

1 cup roughly chopped walnuts

2 (350 g) packages extra-firm silken tofu

1 cup sugar

¾ cup cocoa powder

½ teaspoon salt

1 teaspoon vanilla extract

- Melt the chocolate in a double boiler over low heat

until smooth. Stir in the nondairy milk and maple syrup and remove from the heat. Add the walnuts and coat liberally with a thick chocolate layer.

- Line a cookie sheet with a silicone mat or waxed paper. Spread the chocolate-covered walnuts in an even layer on the prepared cookie sheet. Chill the walnuts in your freezer until you are finished making the mousse.

- To make the mousse, simply blend the tofu, sugar, cocoa powder, salt, and vanilla extract in a food processor or blender until extremely smooth, for about 2 minutes, scraping down the sides as needed.

- Remove the chocolate-covered walnuts from the freezer when they are firm and stir them into the mousse. Spoon into individual dishes and serve very cold. Store in airtight container for up to 1 week in refrigerator.

14. BUTTERNUT POTS DE CRÈME

Tender butternut squash is the base for this incredibly rich chocolate dessert. This makes a fabulous fall-time indulgence. The Pots de Crème can be made up to two days in advance.

2 cups cubed, roasted butternut squash

½ cup coconut sugar or packed brown sugar

¼ cup cocoa powder

¼ cup sorghum flour

1 teaspoon vanilla extract

½ teaspoon salt

Smoked salt for topping

- Preheat oven to 350°F and lightly grease two 4-inch ramekins.

- Puree the squash in food processor until smooth. Add in the sugar, cocoa powder, sorghum flour, vanilla extract, and salt. Blend until all ingredients are well combined, scraping the sides as needed.

- Spoon the mixture into the two ramekins and sprinkle smoked salt onto the custards. Bake for 45 to 50 minutes, or until the sides of the pudding begin to pull away from the ramekins. Serve hot for a softer pudding or serve chilled for a firm dessert. Store in airtight container for up to 1 week in refrigerator.

15. CHOCOLATE SOUP

YIELD: 4 SERVINGS

Somewhere in between pudding and chocolate sauce, this unusual dessert is such a fun choice for dinner parties. Serve this extra-rich dish in very small bowls.

1 cup canned coconut milk, lite or full-fat

¾ cup non dairy milk (unsweetened)

2 teaspoons vanilla extract

⅓ cup sugar

⅛ teaspoon salt

1 tablespoon cocoa powder

½ cup non dairy chocolate, chopped

1 tablespoon cornstarch mixed with 2 tablespoons water

- In a small saucepan, whisk together the coconut milk, non dairy milk, vanilla extract, sugar, salt, and cocoa powder. Heat over medium heat until very hot, but not yet boiling, for about 5 minutes. Stir in the chocolate, and heat just until melted, stirring continuously, making sure not to let the mixture come to a boil. Whisk in the cornstarch slurry and heat for about 3 minutes, stirring constantly, until the mixture has thickened and it coats the back of a spoon. Serve hot in individual bowls garnished with vegan marshmallows or Sweetened Whipped

Coconut Cream and cacao nibs (or mini chocolate chips). Store in airtight container for up to 2 days in refrigerator. Reheat simply by warming over medium-low heat in small saucepan until desired temperature is reached.

16. PEACHY KEEN COBBLER

YIELD: 8 SERVINGS

This cobbler is a perfect way to use up a bunch of fruit, especially when you have a lotta hard peaches rolling around—which tends to happen to me quite often during the summertime (I over purchase and don't want to wait for all of them to ripen!). Any stone fruit can be used; try this recipe with plums or apricots, too!

4 peaches (about 4½ cups) peeled and sliced

½ cup sugar

¼ teaspoon ground allspice

3 tablespoons cornstarch

⅓ cup potato starch

⅓ cup white rice flour

⅓ cup besan/chickpea flour

1 teaspoon xanthan gum

1 teaspoon baking powder

3 tablespoons sugar

6 tablespoons non dairy margarine

¼ cup + 2 tablespoons non dairy milk

1 teaspoon lemon juice

- Preheat oven to 375°F and lightly grease a small stoneware or ceramic baking dish, about 5 × 9 inches.

- In a medium bowl, toss together the peaches, sugar, allspice, and cornstarch. Arrange in the greased baking dish in an even layer.

- In a separate bowl, whisk together the potato starch, white rice flour, besan, xanthan gum, baking powder, and sugar. Cut in the margarine and blend using a pastry blender until even crumbles form. Add in the nondairy milk and lemon juice and stir until smooth.

- Drop by heaping spoonfuls on top of the sliced peaches. Bake for 35 to 40 minutes, or until bubbly and the biscuit top is golden brown on edges. Store in airtight container for up to 1 day.

17.   CHERRY CLAFOUTIS

This recipe is such a perfect use for fresh cherries as this dessert truly accentuates the color and flavor of the short-seasoned fresh fruit. Cherries not in season? Good news: frozen cherries work, too! Thanks to Lydia, who tested for this cookbook, for the tip.

½ block extra-firm tofu, drained but not pressed (about 215 g)

1½ cups besan/chickpea flour

1½ cups non dairy milk

1 teaspoon baking powder

2 tablespoons tapioca flour

¾ cup sugar

¾ teaspoon sea salt

1 teaspoon vanilla extract

2 cups pitted cherries

¼ cup confectioners sugar

- Preheat oven to 350°F and grease an 8-inch cast-iron skillet or glass pie pan with enough margarine to coat.

- Place all the ingredients but the cherries and the confectioner's sugar into a blender and blend until the mixture is uniform and very smooth, scraping down sides as needed. Pour the batter into the prepared pan and then dot evenly with pitted cherries, placing them about ½ inch apart on top of the batter.

- Bake for 50 to 55 minutes, or until a knife inserted into the middle comes out clean. Let cool completely and dust with confectioners sugar before serving. Store in airtight container for up to 2 days in refrigerator.

18. APPLE CRISP

This simple and rustic dessert is as easy to whip up as it is delicious. Serve à la mode for an over-the-top treat.

My favorite type of apple to use in this is Granny Smith, but any crisp variety will do.

5 apples, peeled and sliced ½ to ¼ inch thick

¾ cup brown sugar

½ cup brown rice flour

¼ cup potato starch

1 teaspoon cinnamon

¾ cup certified gluten-free oats

⅓ cup non dairy margarine

- Preheat oven to 375°F. Lightly grease a ceramic baking dish or cake pan, about 8 × 8 inches. Arrange the sliced apples evenly to cover the bottom of the baking dish.

- In a medium bowl, whisk together the brown sugar, brown rice flour, potato starch, cinnamon, and oats. Cut in the margarine using a pastry blender until crumbly. Sprinkle liberally over the apples.

- Bake for 35 to 40 minutes, until golden brown and bubbly. Store in airtight container in refrigerator for up to 2 days.

19. MILLE-FEUILLE

Elegant and classy, this French dessert will make your dinner guests do a double take. Even though it looks complicated, it's really quite easy once you have the puff pastry prepared. Just assemble and serve!

½ recipe <u>Puff Pastry</u>

½ recipe <u>Mascarpone</u>

1 cup confectioners sugar

½ cup <u>Strawberry Preserves</u>

¼ cup cacao nibs

½ cup melted chocolate

Strawberries for garnish

- Preheat oven to 400°F. Line a large baking sheet with parchment or a silicone mat. Roll out the puff pastry into a rectangle about ¼ inch thick. Chill briefly in the freezer, for about 10 minutes, and then carefully cut into even-size rectangles, about 2.5 × 4 inches. Using a flat metal spatula, carefully transfer the puff pastry to the prepared baking sheet, about ½ inch apart. Bake for 15 to 20 minutes, until puffed and golden brown. Let cool completely and then assemble the dessert.

- Mix the Mascarpone with the confectioner's sugar and place into a pastry bag equipped with a star tip. Glaze the tops of each pastry rectangles with Strawberry Preserves and then pipe on circles of the Mascarpone mixture until the top of the rectangle is covered. Sprinkle with cacao nibs. Top with another strawberry preserve–glazed pastry rectangle and again, pipe another layer of mascarpone and sprinkle with cacao nibs. Top with a final rectangle of pastry glazed with strawberry preserves and then drizzle with melted chocolate. Top with a halved strawberry. Chill for 1 hour in refrigerator and then serve cold.

20. SUGAR CRUNCH APPLE PIE

Adding the sugary syrup to the assembled pie is fun and delicious, as it creates a crisp sugar topping, not unlike the candy crunch from crème brûlée.

1 recipe Flakey Classic Piecrust

APPLES

8 medium Granny Smith apples

½ teaspoon cardamom

1 teaspoon cinnamon

½ teaspoon cloves

SAUCE

½ cup non dairy margarine

4 tablespoons superfine brown rice flour

¼ cup water

1 cup packed brown sugar

- Prepare the pie dough according to recipe directions, divide into two disks and chill for 2 hours in your refrigerator. Core and peel the apples. Slice thinly and lightly toss with cardamom, cinnamon, and cloves.

- Once pie crusts are chilled, roll out one section of dough in between two sheets of parchment paper to a ¼ inch thickness. Use the parchment paper to help flip the rolled out crust into a lightly greased pie pan. Cut off excess dough and reserve.

- Heap the sliced apples into a mound on top of the crust in the pie pan.

- Take the second chilled dough disk and roll to same thickness in between two sheets of parchment paper. As you did with the first crust, use the parchment to help you flip the dough over on top of the mound of apples. If any dough rips, simply use your fingertips dipped in water to help seal it back together. Build up the sides with excess dough to form a shallow wall as the outer crust. Make a few ¼-inch-wide slits in the top crust to vent.

- Whisk the ingredients for the sauce together into a 2-quart saucepan on medium heat and let it come to a boil, while stirring occasionally. After it has come to a boil, reduce heat to simmer and let cook for 2 minutes. Remove the sauce from the heat.

- Preheat your oven to 425°F. Pour the sugar mixture on top of pie crust, aiming mostly for the slits in the center, and allow any excess to drip over sides. Once all sauce has been added to the pie use a pastry brush to gently brush the remaining syrup evenly over the pie.

- Bake for 15 minutes, then reduce oven temp to 350°F and bake for an additional 35 to 45 minutes. Remove from oven, and let cool for at least 2 hours before serving. Store in airtight container for up to 2 days.

21.   BANANA CREAM PIE

YIELD: 10 SERVINGS

Up until the Great Depression, bananas were practically unheard of in desserts. Apparently, it was the frugalness of using the overripe bananas that led to incorporating them into sweets. With its rich, cream filling, this pie is the very opposite of frugal! It is best enjoyed right after cooling as the bananas tend to discolor after a day or so; one very good way to remedy this is to freeze the pie immediately after it cools and serve mostly frozen.

½ recipe Flakey Classic Pie Crust

FILLING

¾ cup sugar

⅓ cup white rice flour

¼ teaspoon salt

2 cups non dairy milk

3 tablespoons cornstarch mixed with 3 tablespoons water

2 tablespoons non dairy margarine

2 teaspoons vanilla extract

4 large bananas

- Preheat oven to 400°F.

- Prepare the pie crust according to recipe directions and then blind bake in oven for 10 minutes. Reduce oven temperature to 350°F.

- In a 2-quart saucepan, whisk together the sugar, white rice flour, salt, nondairy milk, and cornstarch slurry. Add the margarine and vanilla extract. Heat over medium heat until the mixture comes to a boil, stirring constantly. Let cook for 1 minute, still stirring constantly, until the mixture thickens considerably.

- Slice the bananas into the baked pie crust forming an even layer. Pour the hot sugar mixture over the bananas to cover and bake in preheated oven for 15 minutes. Remove from oven and let cool. Chill and serve with fresh banana slices and Sweetened Whipped Coconut Cream. Store in airtight container in refrigerator for up to 2 days.

22. KEY LIME PIE

YIELD: **10**
SERVINGS

Sweet yet sour, this creamy pie will transport you straight to the Florida Keys. I recommend using bottled key lime juice for ease and availability.

CRUST

1 cup gluten-free cookie crumbs (use hard cookie such as Pizzelles, Cinnamon Graham Crackers, Vanilla Wafers, etc.)

1 cup ground pecans

3 tablespoons sugar

2 tablespoons ground chia seed mixed with 4 tablespoons water

1 tablespoon coconut oil

FILLING

1 (350 g) package extra-firm silken tofu

1 cup key lime juice

1 cup canned full-fat coconut milk

½ cup coconut cream from the top of a can of full-fat coconut milk

1 cup sugar

2 tablespoons confectioners sugar

¾ teaspoons salt

¼ cup besan/chickpea flour

¼ cup white rice flour

2 tablespoons cornstarch

1 teaspoon lime zest, plus more for topping

- Preheat oven to 375°F.

- Mix together all the crust ingredients, in order given, and press into a standard-size pie pan.

- In the bowl of a food processor, place the filling ingredients, pulsing a few times after each addition, until smooth. Be sure to scrape down sides as needed.

• Pour the filling mixture into the crust and carefully transfer to the middle rack of your oven. Bake for 20 minutes. Reduce heat to 300°F and bake for an additional 40 to 45 minutes, until very lightly golden brown on edges. Let cool at room temperature and then chill in refrigerator overnight. Top with lime zest and Sweetened Whipped Coconut Cream. Store in airtight container in refrigerator for up to 2 days.

23. CHERRY PIE BARS

YIELD: 8 SERVINGS

The taste is just like cherry pie but these little bars are actually pretty good for you! I recommend seeking out the highest-quality dried cherries (organic, unsulphured, with no added sugar) for these for the most authentic cherry-pie flavor.

2 cups raw cashews

1 cup dried cherries (not sweetened)

½ teaspoon salt

10 Medjool dates

- In a food processor, combine the cashews, cherries, and salt and blend until coarsely crumbled. Add in the dates and pulse until finely crumbled and the mixture easily comes together and stays together when squeezed.

- Shape the mixture into individual bars by shaping into a tight disk, or square, and then cutting gently with knife. Wrap individually in plastic wrap or foil. Alternatively, shape into balls for bite-size snacking. Store in airtight container in refrigerator for up to 2 weeks.

24. CHERRY CHOCOLATE ALMOND SNACK BARS

Like a crunchy granola bar, these chocolate bars are a great pick-me-up when your energy is down. Be sure to use only kasha (toasted buckwheat) that is brown in color, rather than greenish. Kasha is usually located next to untoasted buckwheat groats, oftentimes in the bulk or natural foods sections.

1½ cups kasha (toasted buckwheat kernels), soaked for 2 hours

⅓ cup + 2 tablespoons cocoa powder

2 tablespoons chia seed

½ cup maple syrup

3 tablespoons date sugar

⅔ cup almond flour

½ teaspoon salt

½ cup dried cherries (not sweetened)

¼ teaspoon coconut or olive oil

- Preheat oven to 300°F. Line a baking tray with parchment paper.

- Drain the soaked kasha completely. In a large bowl, combine all of the ingredients except for the oil. Use the ¼ teaspoon coconut oil to grease clean hands and gently pat down the mixture into a rectangle, about ¼ to ½ inch thick. Bake for 30 minutes. Remove from oven, gently cut into squares using a spatula (but don't separate) and continue to bake for an additional 20 minutes. Let cool completely and then break into individual bars. Store in airtight container for up to 1 week.

25. BLUEBERRY BLIZZARD MILKSHAKE

YIELD: 1 SERVING

Blueberries are full of antioxidants and lend a beautiful blue hue to this milk shake. And that's not the only healthy ingredient: it's sweetened with bananas.

½ cup fresh or frozen blueberries

1½ peeled and frozen bananas

1 teaspoon vanilla extract

1 cup non dairy milk (almond is best)

- Place all the ingredients into a blender and blend until completely smooth. Serve immediately with a thick straw.

26. SUGAR PLUMS

YIELD:
24
SUGAR
PLUMS

These little gems have become well known from their very important cameo in the classic Christmas tale, and, even though they may conjure up images of sugar-covered plums in your mind, they actually have never contained any plums at all. "Plum" used to be a popular way to describe any dried fruit, but sugar plums usually contained a mixture of dates, apricots, or figs to achieve their sweetness.

1 cup raw almonds

1 teaspoon lemon or orange zest

½ cup chopped dried figs

½ cup chopped dried dates

½ teaspoon cinnamon

¼ teaspoon nutmeg

Dash ground cloves

2 tablespoons agave

½ cup confectioners sugar for dusting

- Preheat oven to 400°F and spread the almonds in an even layer on a cookie sheet. Bake for 7 minutes, or until fragrant.

- Place almonds, zest, figs, dates, cinnamon, nutmeg, and cloves into a food processor and pulse until crumbly. Add in the agave, 1 tablespoon at a time, and pulse again, until the mixture comes together easily. Pinch into 1-inch balls and roll in the confectioner's sugar. Store in airtight container for up to 1 week.

27. CANDIED ORANGE PEELS

Candied orange peels are so nice to have for decorative purposes or to add a little zing to a dessert, like in my Florentines. This recipe also works nicely with lemon or lime peels, which add a nice color variation to the mix.

4 navel oranges

1½ cups sugar

¾ cup water

Dash salt

- Remove the peels from the oranges by slicing through the peel and quartering it, without puncturing the fruit. Gently cut off the top and bottom of the orange and then carefully peel the orange peel, leaving behind the pith and fruit.

Reserve pith and fruit for another use (these make fantastic juicing oranges).

- Lay one section of peel flat onto a cutting area, light-side-up. Slice the peel into thin, even strips, about ¼ inch wide.

- Place the peels into a medium saucepan and cover with 1 inch of water and salt very lightly. Boil for 20 minutes, and then drain. Briefly place onto clean kitchen towel to dry.

- Drain the saucepan and then wipe dry. Place the drained peels, sugar, water, and salt into the pot and cook over medium heat. Cook until the mixture reaches 235°F on a candy thermometer (or Soft Ball Stage if using the Cold Water Method). Spread in an even layer onto a waxed paper–covered cookie sheet or silicone mat. Let harden for 2 hours, and for up to 12 hours before transferring to airtight container. Store for up to 1 month.

28. SOUR FRUIT JELLIES

These jelly candies are a touch softer than traditional gumdrops. They actually taste more like fruit snacks made for children's lunches.

¾ cup white grape juice

⅓ cup fruit pectin

½ teaspoon baking soda

1 cup sugar

1 cup agave

1 to 2 drops food coloring, any color

¼ teaspoon citric acid

⅓ cup turbinado sugar

- Line an 8 × 8-inch pan snugly with aluminum foil and spray generously with nonstick spray or grease with margarine.

- In a small saucepan, over medium heat, warm the grape juice, pectin, and baking soda just until boiling. Once boiling, reduce heat to lowest setting, stirring occasionally.

- In a 2-quart saucepan, whisk together the sugar and agave and cook over medium heat, until it reaches 265°F on a candy thermometer (or Hard Ball Stage if using the Cold Water Method). Be sure to stir occasionally while this mixture is cooking, and, once the sugar dissolves, brush down the sides with a wet pastry brush to remove any crystals.

- After the sugar mixture has reached 265°F, stir in the grape juice mixture along with the desired shade of food coloring. You can easily separate these into various colors by pouring the mixture into separate bowls and coloring each a different color. Pour into the prepared pan (or pans if making multiple colors) and chill in refrigerator overnight. Remove from refrigerator and cut into shapes using a very small cookie cutters. Mix the citric acid and turbinado sugar in a small bowl and dip the cut candies to coat. Store in refrigerator in airtight container for up to 1 month.

29. CHOCOLATE SILK PIE

YIELD: 10 SERVINGS

This is one of my favorite desserts to bring to potlucks because of its simplicity and versatility. The secret ingredient is silken tofu, which creates a base that's both firm and silky. Top each individual piece with Sweetened Whipped Coconut Cream just before serving.

½ recipe Flakey Classic Piecrust

2 (350 g) packages extra-firm silken tofu

2 teaspoons vanilla extract

2 tablespoons cocoa powder (I like extra-dark)

½ cup sugar

1½ cups chopped non dairy chocolate or chocolate chips

- Preheat oven to 400°F.

- Prepare the pie crust according to recipe directions and roll out in between two sheets of parchment paper until about ¼ inch thick.

- Flip over the parchment to gently place the crust into a standard-size glass pie pan. Fold or flute the crust and pierce bottom several times evenly with fork. Bake for 20 minutes, or until light golden brown. Remove from oven.

- To prepare the filling, blend the tofu, vanilla extract, cocoa powder, and sugar in a food processor until completely smooth, scraping down sides as needed.

- In a double boiler, melt the chocolate and drizzle into the tofu mixture and blend until completely incorporated. Spread filling into baked pie shell and let cool at room temperature for 1 hour before transferring to the refrigerator to chill until slightly firm, 4 hours up to overnight. Store in airtight container in refrigerator for up to 3 days.

30. SKY-HIGH PEANUT BUTTER PIE

YIELD: 10 SERVINGS

If you love peanut butter you're going to flip over this pie. Rich peanut butter and chocolate combine for a luscious base, while fluffy coconut cream gives the pie its name. You can also switch this up and use almond or cashew butter if you have a peanut allergy.

½ recipe Flakey Classic Piecrust

4 ounces semi-sweet chocolate

3 (350 g) packages firm silken tofu

2 cups creamy peanut butter

2 cups confectioners sugar

3 tablespoons ground chia seed

½ teaspoon sea salt

1 recipe Sweetened Whipped Coconut Cream

2 ounces non dairy chocolate chips or chunks, melted, for drizzling

¼ cup crushed roasted and salted peanuts

- Preheat oven to 400°F and prepare the pie crust according to recipe directions. Roll out in between two sheets of parchment until ¼ inch thick. Drape over a deep-dish pie pan and press down evenly to cover. Flute edges and bake for 20 minutes, or until lightly golden brown. Remove from oven and place on wire rack to cool. Sprinkle 4 ounces of the chocolate chips evenly onto the piecrust and let rest for 5 minutes. Spread the melted chocolate, using a silicone spatula, to coat the inside of the pie crust. Let cool completely until chocolate is rehardened—once the crust is at room temperature, place in the refrigerator to speed up the process.

- In a food processor combine the tofu, peanut butter, sugar, chia seed, and salt. Blend until completely smooth, for about 5 minutes. Spread into the prepared pie crust, and freeze for at least 3 hours. Transfer to refrigerator and chill overnight. Before serving, top with whipped coconut cream and drizzle with chocolate. Sprinkle with crushed peanuts. Store in an airtight container in the refrigerator for up to 2 days.

31. PECAN PIE

YIELD: 10 SERVINGS

The first time I tasted Pecan Pie, I was smitten. Even today when I get around one, it takes a bit of restraint for me to stop eating the whole darn thing! Best to share with others, or just make two pies, and save yourself the heartache.

½ recipe Flakey Classic Piecrust

2 tablespoons flaxseed meal

¼ cup water

1¼ cups packed brown sugar

2 tablespoons superfine brown rice flour, or white rice flour

2 teaspoons vanilla extract

½ cup melted non dairy margarine

1½ cups chopped pecan

- Preheat oven to 400°F. Prepare the pie crust according to recipe directions and press into a standard-size pie pan, making the crust slightly shorter than the top edge of the pan. Flute or use a spoon to make a design in the top of the crust.

- In a large bowl, stir together flaxseed meal and water and let set for 5 minutes, until gelled. Transfer to a mixing bowl and whip on high speed using a whisk attachment for 1 minute (or using elbow grease and a whisk), until fluffy. Add the sugar, brown rice flour, vanilla extract, and margarine. Fold in 1 cup of the chopped pecans. Stir well. Spoon filling into unbaked crust and then top with remaining chopped pecans.

- Bake for 35 to 40 minutes, until crust is golden brown and filling is bubbly. Carefully remove from the oven and let cool completely, for at least 4 hours, before serving. Store in airtight container in refrigerator for up to 2 days.

32. CHERRY ALMOND BISCOTTI

YIELD: 20 BISCOTTI

This tart and slightly sweet cookie complements tea or coffee beautifully with its fruity notes. Not only is it pleasing to the taste buds, your eyes are in for a treat with deep red cherries studded throughout.

2 tablespoons flaxseed meal

4 tablespoons water

⅓ cup non dairy margarine

¾ cup sugar

1½ teaspoons almond extract

½ teaspoon salt

2 teaspoons baking powder

1 cup sorghum flour

¾ cup brown rice flour

½ cup potato starch

1 teaspoon xanthan gum

¼ cup non dairy milk

1 cup dried cherries

- Preheat oven to 325°F. Combine the flaxseed meal and water into a bowl and let rest for 5 minutes, until gelled.

- In a large bowl, cream together the margarine and sugar until smooth. Add the prepared flaxseed meal, almond extract, and salt.

- In a separate bowl, whisk together the baking powder, sorghum flour, brown rice flour, potato starch, and xanthan gum. Gradually incorporate into the sugar mixture. Add non dairy milk, 1 tablespoon at a time, until a soft dough forms. It should be just dry enough to handle and shape into two balls. Add a touch more sorghum flour or milk to create the right consistency. The dough shouldn't crumble apart, but it also shouldn't be too sticky. Fold in the dried cherries until even distributed.

- Directly on an ungreased cookie sheet, shape the cookie dough into two ovals, about 2.5 inches wide and 1.25 inches tall. Bake in preheated oven for about 30 minutes, until lightly golden on edges. Let cool and then slice cookies diagonally. Place freshly cut cookies on their sides and bake an additional 8 minutes. Turn cookies over and bake another 8 minutes. And one more time … flip, and bake a final 8 minutes. Let cool completely before enjoying. Store in airtight container for up to 3 weeks.

33. MARBLE BISCOTTI

YIELD: 18 BISCOTTI

Chocolate and vanilla mingle in this delightful-looking cookie. Dip into piping hot coffee or hot chocolate for the ultimate biscotti experience. If you're sharing, these make great gifts once you wrap them up in shiny plastic wrap and adorn them with a bow, especially when paired with your favorite blend of coffee.

3 tablespoons flaxseed meal

6 tablespoons water

½ cup sugar

½ cup non dairy margarine

½ teaspoon vanilla extract

1 cup sorghum flour

¾ cup brown rice flour

½ cup potato starch

¼ cup tapioca flour

1 teaspoon xanthan gum

1½ teaspoons baking powder

½ teaspoon salt

½ cup non dairy chocolate chips, melted, plus 1 cup chocolate chips, melted, for drizzling

- Preheat oven to 325°F.

- In a small bowl, combine flaxseed meal with water and let rest until gelled, for about 5 minutes. In large mixing bowl, cream together the sugar and the margarine. Add the prepared flaxseed meal and vanilla extract and mix well. In a separate bowl, combine the sorghum flour, brown rice flour, potato starch, tapioca flour, xanthan gum, baking powder, and salt. Stir well to evenly incorporate.

- Slowly combine the flour mixture with the margarine mixture until clumpy. Divide dough into two sections, leaving half in the mixing bowl and setting the rest aside. Gently stir in the ½ cup melted chocolate chips with one-half of the dough until very well combined, scraping bowl as needed.

- Now you will have two sections of dough: one chocolate and one vanilla. Shape the vanilla dough into two balls. Shape the chocolate mixture into two balls as well. Then, roll each section into long ropes, so that you have four long ropes of both chocolate and vanilla—about 10 inches long each.

- Working on an ungreased baking sheet, place one chocolate rope and one vanilla rope side by side and then twist over one another, pressing together to form a flat log about 3 inches by 10 inches and then repeat with other two ropes.

- Bake for 28 minutes, until lightly golden brown on edges, and then remove from the oven and place onto a wire rack to let completely cool. Using a serrated knife, slice diagonally into 3 × 1-inch cookies and place freshly cut cookies on their sides on the cookie sheet.

- Bake cookies for 10 minutes. Flip and bake for 10 more minutes. Flip one more time and bake for 5 more minutes. Let cool completely and then drizzle or coat one side with melted chocolate.

- Store in airtight container for up to 1 month.

34. ULTIMATE FUDGY BROWNIES

YIELD: 12 BROWNIES

These brownies boast a crispy, flaky, paper-thin layer atop a chewy, gooey perfect square of brownie bliss. Even though these brownies are pretty delicious all by their lonesome, they do take kindly to a thin layer of frosting on top, too. Try them topped with Fluffy Chocolate Frosting or Caramel Frosting for an extra-indulgent treat!

¾ cup superfine brown rice flour

¼ cup almond meal

¼ cup potato starch

¼ cup sorghum flour

1 teaspoon xanthan gum

½ teaspoon baking soda

1 teaspoon salt

3 cups chopped non dairy chocolate or chocolate chips

1 cup sugar

¼ cup non dairy margarine

½ cup strong coffee

2 tablespoons ground chia seed mixed with 5 tablespoons hot water

1 teaspoon vanilla extract

1 cup non dairy white chocolate chips (optional)

- Preheat oven 325°F and lightly grease a 9 × 13-inch metal pan.

- In a large electric mixing bowl, whisk together the superfine brown rice flour, almond meal, potato starch, sorghum flour, xanthan gum, baking soda, and salt.

- Place the chocolate chips into a large heat-safe bowl.

- In a 2-quart saucepan over medium heat, combine the sugar, margarine, and
  ¼ cup of the coffee and bring to a boil, stirring often. Once boiling, immediately remove from the heat and pour the hot sugar mixture directly onto the chocolate chips, stirring quickly to combine

thoroughly. Transfer to the mixing bowl containing the flour mixture along with the prepared chia gel and vanilla extract and mix on medium-high speed until smooth. Add in the additional ¼ cup coffee and mix well. If you're using them, fold in white chocolate chips.

- Spread the batter in the prepared baking pan—the batter will be tacky. Bake for 45 to 50 minutes. Let cool completely before cutting into squares and serving. Store in airtight container for up to 3 days.

35. BLONDIES

Blondies are lighter than brownies in taste, texture, and color but still bear a delicious resemblance to their chocolate pals. Try these topped with Peanut Butter Banana Ice Cream.

2 tablespoons flaxseed meal

4 tablespoons water

⅓ cup coconut palm sugar

1 teaspoon vanilla extract

1 cup brown rice flour

½ cup almond meal

¼ cup potato starch

1 teaspoon xanthan gum

½ teaspoon salt

½ cup non dairy margarine

1 tablespoon coconut oil

1½ cups non dairy white chocolate chips or pieces

½ cup non dairy mini chocolate chips

- Preheat oven to 350°F. Lightly grease an 8 × 8-inch baking pan.

- In a small bowl, combine the flaxseed meal and water and let rest until gelled, for about 5 minutes. Stir in the coconut palm sugar and vanilla extract. In a separate bowl, whisk together the brown rice flour, almond meal, potato starch, xanthan gum, and salt.

- Over a double boiler, on medium-low heat, melt the margarine, coconut oil, and white chocolate until smooth. Remove from heat. Stir white chocolate mixture into the flour mixture along with the flaxseed meal mixture until a batter forms. Fold in the mini chocolate chips. Press the batter into the prepared baking pan and bake for 27 minutes, or until golden brown on edges. Let cool completely, for at least 2 hours, before serving. Store in airtight container for up to 1 week.

36. LIGHTEN UP LEMON BARS

YIELD: 16 BARS

These are a lightened-up version of traditional lemon bars, leaving out the eggs and butter and opting for plant-based ingredients instead. Agar can easily be sourced at local health food stores or Asian markets. If you can only source agar bars or flakes, simply run them through a spice grinder until powdered.

CRUST

2 tablespoons flaxseed meal

4 tablespoons water

1½ cups almond meal

¼ teaspoon salt

3 tablespoons sugar

FILLING

2 cups water

1½ tablespoons agar powder

1¼ cups sugar

1 cup freshly squeezed lemon juice (about 6 lemons' worth)

1 drop natural yellow food coloring

¼ cup cornstarch dissolved completely in ¼ cup water

Confectioner's sugar, for dusting

- Preheat oven to 400°F.

- In a small bowl, mix the flaxseed meal with the water until gelled, for about
  5 minutes. In a medium bowl, whisk together the rest of the crust ingredients and then massage the prepared flaxseed meal into the almond meal mixture until well blended. Press crust into a lightly greased 8 × 8- inch baking pan. Bake for 12 to 15 minutes, until golden brown on edges. Remove from oven and let cool while you make the filling.

- To make the filling, bring the 2 cups water and agar

powder to a boil over medium heat, stirring constantly with a whisk. Let boil for 3 to 5 minutes, until thickened and all agar has dissolved. (Be sure that all agar has dissolved or your lemon bars won't set correctly.) Stir in the sugar, lemon juice, food coloring, and cornstarch slurry. Continue to cook over medium heat, bringing back up to a boil. Let boil for about 3 minutes, until thickened. Pour the mixture on top of the crust and chill immediately on a flat surface in your refrigerator. Chill 2 hours, or until firm. Cut into squares. Dust with confectioners sugar before serving. Store in refrigerator for up to 1 week.

37. FLAKEY CLASSIC PIE CRUST

YIELD: 2 STANDARD-SIZE PIE CRUSTS, OR ENOUGH FOR 1 LATTICE-TOPPED OR COVERED PIE

This piecrust is a staple in this chapter. With a flaky, buttery consistency, it truly does make a pie stand out!

1 cup superfine brown rice flour

¾ cup white rice flour

½ cup potato starch

½ cup tapioca flour

1½ teaspoons xanthan gum

½ teaspoon baking powder

3 tablespoons sugar

10 tablespoons cold non dairy margarine

3 tablespoons lemon juice

½ cup ice-cold water

- In a large bowl, whisk together the superfine brown rice flour, white rice flour, potato starch, tapioca flour, xanthan gum, baking powder, and sugar.

- Drop the margarine into the flour mixture by tablespoons. Use fingers or pastry blender to quickly mix into an even crumble. Using a large fork, stir in the lemon juice and cold water until a soft dough forms. If the dough seems too sticky, add a touch more brown rice flour. Wrap in plastic wrap and chill in the freezer for 15 minutes, or refrigerator for at least 1 hour before using.

- Keeps tightly covered in refrigerator for up to 1 week, and frozen for up to 3 months.

38. PUFF PASTRY

The key to this super-flakey pastry is keeping the dough cold! Be sure to chill adequately between rotations to ensure a workable dough. I also recommend chilling all ingredients before getting started.

$\frac{3}{4}$ cup superfine brown rice flour

$\frac{3}{4}$ cup white rice flour

$\frac{2}{3}$ cup potato starch

$\frac{1}{3}$ cup tapioca flour

2 teaspoons xanthan gum

$1\frac{1}{4}$ cups very cold non dairy margarine

$\frac{1}{2}$ cup ice-cold water

- In a large bowl, whisk together the brown rice flour, $\frac{1}{2}$ cup of the white rice flour, potato starch, tapioca flour, and xanthan gum. Drop in the margarine by the spoonful. Using clean hands, quickly cut the margarine into the flour until the mixture resembles pebbles.

- Add in the cold water and mix quickly to form a slightly sticky dough. Punch down into the bowl to flatten the dough and sprinkle with 2 tablespoons white rice flour; pat into the dough to make it less sticky. Flip and repeat with the additional 2 tablespoons white rice flour.

- Chill the dough for 20 minutes in the freezer.

- In between two sheets of parchment paper, roll out the dough into a rectangle about 5 × 9 inches. Use a straight edge to square up the edges, forming a solid rectangle. Work quickly so that the dough stays cold!

- Fold the dough into thirds (like folding a letter) and rotate a quarter of a turn. Use the parchment to help fold the dough over evenly. Roll it out again into another rectangle 5 × 9 inches. Fold it into thirds once again. Wrap loosely in parchment and chill in the freezer for an additional 20 minutes.

- Repeat the steps again, exactly as described above. Wrap and chill the puff pastry until ready to use. When working with the pastry, be sure not to roll it out too thin, ⅓ to ½ of an inch is just right.

- Use as directed in recipes calling for puff pastry. To deepen the color of the pastry, mix 2 teaspoons cornstarch with ½ cup water—bring to a boil over medium heat and cook until translucent. Brush a little of the paste onto the surface before baking. Keeps frozen for up to 1 month.

CPSIA information can be obtained
at www.ICGtesting.com
Printed in the USA
LVHW051653010621
689062LV00009B/623

9 781802 681130